BACH

Sleepers, Wake!

(WACHET AUF, RUFT UNS DIE STIMME)

Cantata for soprano, tenor, & bass soli,
SATB & orchestra
(Cantata No 140)

The piano accompaniment arranged by Ebenezer Prout
The English translation by Miss G. E. Troutbeck

Order No: NOV 070024

NOVELLO PUBLISHING LIMITED

CANTATA No. 140

ORIGINAL SCORE

1. Strings, 2 Oboes, Taille*, Horn, Continuo
2. Continuo
3. Violino piccolo, Continuo
4. Violins I., II., Viola (*Unis.*), Continuo
5. Strings, Continuo
6. Oboe, Continuo
7. Strings, 2 Oboes, Taille, Horn, Continuo

* *Taille* = the tenor voice of a family of instruments, in this case the ***Oboe da Caccia***, or modern ***English Horn***.

The Horn is used only in unison with the Sopranos, and may be omitted.

The Violino piccolo solo is played on the ordinary Violin.

PREFATORY NOTE.

THE present work, one of the finest of the one hundred and ninety Church Cantatas of Bach which are in existence, was composed during his residence in Leipzig. It was written for the twenty-seventh Sunday after Trinity; and as this Sunday occurs only when Easter falls unusually early, it is known that the work must date either from 1731 or from 1742. Spitta pronounces in favour of the earlier year: the late William Rust, in the preface to the Bach Society's edition of the score, shows good reason for believing that it was not written till 1742.

The Cantata is scored for strings, two oboes, *taille* (*i.e.*, an alto oboe, of the same pitch as the modern *cor anglaise*), and organ. There are also among the original orchestral parts, which are preserved in the Thomas-Schule at Leipzig, parts for bassoon, which doubles the bass throughout, and for a horn, which plays the choral in the first and last numbers, in unison with the soprano chorus.

The "Continuo" part is fully figured throughout, and has been of much assistance to the Editor in arranging the accompaniment, especially in the two duets, in which the orchestral instruments have only the outer parts of the harmony. It is impossible to say exactly in which positions Bach himself filled up the harmonies on the organ, his figuring has been closely followed in this arrangement, in which, of course, the orchestral parts are also included. Had the Editor been writing a separate organ part, he would in many passages have taken a different position for the harmony. This could not be done in the present vocal score without obscuring too much the progression of Bach's instrumental parts.

The Cantata was first published, in full score, in the first part of Winterfield's *Evangelische Kirchengesänge* (Leipzig, 1847).

EBENEZER PROUT.

LONDON, *March*, 1901.

SLEEPERS WAKE! FOR NIGHT IS FLYING
CANTATA
for the Sunday next before Advent.

English version by
Georgina E. Troutbeck.

J. S. Bach.

A
SOPRANO.
Sleep - - - ers wake! for
ALTO.
Sleep - ers wake! sleep - ers
TENOR.
Sleep - ers
BASS.
A
Vl.
Ob.
Vl.
Ob.
B
night is fly - - - - - - -
wake! night swift is fly - ing, night swift is
wake! sleep - ers wake! night swift is fly - - ing, is
Sleep - ers wake! sleep - ers wake! night swift is
B
- ing
fly - ing
fly - ing
fly - ing

C
f
The watch - - - men on
f
The watch on thy walls
f
The watch on thy walls
f
The watch on thy
C
mf
thy walls are cry - - - - - - ing:
D
loud are cry - ing a - loud are cry - - - ing, a - loud are cry - ing:
loud are cry - - - ing, the watch on thy walls loud are cry - ing:
walls loud are cry - - ing, up - on thy walls a - loud are cry - ing:
D
f

E
f
Thou
A - wake,
A - wake,
A - wake,
mf
ci - - - ty of Je - - -
a - wake, a - wake, a - wake Je - ru - sa - lem, a - wake,
a - wake, a - wake, a - wake Je - ru - sa - lem,
a - wake, a - wake, a - wake Je - ru - sa - lem, a - wake,
F
- ru - - - sa - - - lem!
a - wake Je - ru - - sa - lem, a - wake, a - wake Je -
a - wake Je - ru - - sa - lem, a - wake, a - wake Je - ru - sa -
a - wake Je - ru - sa - - lem, a - wake, a - wake Je -

-ru- -sa-lem!
-lem Je-ru-sa-lem!
-ru- -sa-lem!
Vl.
Ob.
Vl.
f
Ob.
Vl.
mf
Ob.
Ob.
cresc.
tr
ff

G
f
Hear ye now ere
Hear ye now, hear ye
Hear ye
G
Vl.
Ob.
mf
Vl.
Ob.
H
comes the morn - - - - -
now, ere com-eth morn-ing, ere com - - eth
now, hear ye now, ere com-eth morn - ing, com-eth
Hear ye now, hear ye now, ere com - eth
H
- ing,
morn-ing,
morn- ing,
morn - ing,

I
The mid - - - night call
The mid-night call of so -
The mid-night call of so -
The mid-night call of
K
of so - - - lemn
- - lemn warn - ing, the mid-night call
- - lemn warn - ing, the mid-night call
so - - - lemn warn - - ing, the mid-night
warn - - - - - ing:
— of so - - lemn warn-ing:
the mid-night call of so - - lemn warn - ing:
call, the mid-night call of so - lemn warn - ing:

L
Where
Where, where,
Where, where,
Where, where,
are ye, O wise
where, where, where are ye, O ye wise virgins, where
where, where, where are ye, O ye wise vir - gins, where
where, where, where are ye, where, where, where are ye, where are ye,
M
vir - - - gins, where?
where are ye O ye wise vir - gins, where are ye, O · ye wise
are ye, where are ye O wise vir - gins, where are ye, where are
O ye wise vir - - - gins, where are ye O ye wise

Vir - gins, where, where?
ye wise Vir - gins, where, where?
Vir - gins, where, where?
cresc.

N
mf
Be - - - - hold
Be - hold, be - hold the Bride - groom
Behold, be - hold, be - hold, be -
Behold, behold the Bride - groom comes, behold!
ff
tr
mf
the Bride - - - - groom
comes, be - hold, be - hold, be - hold! the Bride - groom
- hold, be - hold! the Bride - groom comes, be - hold, be -
the Bride - groom comes, be - hold! the Bride - groom
O
comes
comes, behold, be - hold!
- hold, behold, be - hold!
comes, behold, be - hold!
f

P
cresc.
A - - - rise! and
cresc.
A - rise, a - rise! and take your lamps, a-rise, a -
cresc.
A-rise, a - rise, a - rise, a - rise, a-rise
cresc.
A-rise, a-rise! and take your lamps, a-rise and take your
P
mf
Q
take your lamps
- rise a - rise! and take your lamps, a - rise, a -
and take your lamps a - rise, a - rise, a - rise, a -
lamps, a - rise! and take your lamps, a - rise, a -
Q
R
mf
- rise! Al - - - le -
- rise!
- rise!
R
f
mf

S
-lu-ia, al-le-lu - ia,
mf
Al - - - - - - le -
S
T
al-le-lu-ia,
al-le-lu - ia,
tr
al-le-lu-ia,
-lu-ia, al-le-lu - ia,
Al - - - - - - le-
T
al - le - lu - ia,
al - le - lu-
al-le-lu-ia,
al-le-lu - ia,
al-le-lu - ia,
-lu-ia, al-le-lu - ia,
al-le-lu - ia,
8

U
mf
al - le - lu -
-ia,
al - le - lu - ia, al - le - lu - ia,
al - le - lu - ia, al - le - lu - ia, al - le - lu -
U
8
V
-ia!
al - le - lu - ia, al - le - lu - ia!
al - le - lu - ia!
-ia, al - le - lu - ia!
V
Ob.
Vl.
f
W
f
your -
f
your -
f
yourselves prepare,
f
yourselves pre -
Ob.
Vl.
W
Ob.
mf
8

-selves pre - - - - - pare,

-selves pre-pare, your-selves pre-pare, pre - pare, pre -

yourselves pre-pare, yourselves pre - pare, pre -

-pare, yourselves pre - pare, yourselves pre - pare, pre -

-pare, yourselves pre - pare,

-pare, yourselves pre - pare,

-pare, yourselves pre - pare,

f

X

f Your Lord draws

f your - selves pre - - pare, your - selves pre - -

f your - selves pre - - pare, your - selves pre -

f yourselves pre - pare, your Lord

X

mf

near,
-pare, yourselves pre - pare, your Lord draws near, yourselves pre -
-pare, yourselves pre - pare, your Lord draws near, yourselves pre -
draws near, yourselves pre - pare, your Lord draws near, yourselves pre -
-pare, your Lord draws near,
-pare, your Lord draws near,
-pare, your Lord draws near,
cresc.

Y
f
He, bids you to
He, He, He bids you to His mar - riage -
He, He, He bids you to His
He, He, He bids you to His mar - riage -
Y
mf
Z
His mar - - - riage - - - feast
feast, He bids you to His mar - riage, His mar-riage feast, He
mar - - riage feast, to His mar - riage - feast He bids you
feast, He bids you to His mar - riage - - feast, He bids
Z

bids you to His mar - - riage - feast.
to His mar-riage-feast, His mar - riage - feast.
you to His mar - - riage - feast.
f
cresc.
tr
ff

RECITATIVE.

TENOR.
He comes, He comes, the Bride-groom comes! and Zi - on's
Org.
daughter shall rejoice, He hast'neth hi-ther from the mountains, our land shall hear His voice
The Bridegroom comes, and like a roe or a youth-ful hart up-on the lof-ty Hills He
treads, your soul with heav'n - ly food He feeds. A - rise, and lin-ger not! With
songs of glad-ness greet Him; lo! 'tis He! Come ye forth to meet Him.

AIR. (DUET.)
Adagio. ♪ = 72.
poco cresc.
mf
poco dim.
SOPRANO.
mp
a
I seek Thee, my Life,
I
BASS.
mf
Be - hold Me, thy Life,
a
p
poco cresc.
seek Thee, my Life, I seek Thee, my
mp
Be-hold Me, thy Life, Be - hold Me,
poco cresc.

poco cresc.
Life, my Life! I tar - - - ry, I
thy Life, thy Life, Be-hold Me,
p
poco cresc.
mp
b
tar - - ry with lamp e-ver burning; I seek Thee, my Life,
mf
Be-hold Me, Behold Me, Be -
b
dim.
p
poco cresc.
mp
I seek Thee, my Life, I
- hold Me, thy Life, Be- hold Me, thy Life,
poco cresc.

poco cresc.
tar - - - ry, I tar - - - - -
poco cresc.
Be - hold Me, Be - hold Me,
p poco cresc.
poco dim.
- - - - - - ry, with
poco dim.
Be - hold Me, thy Life, Be - hold Me, thy
poco dim.
cresc.
f
C
lamp e - ver burn - ing, with lamp e - ver burn-ing I
f
Life, Be - hold Me, thy Life,
C
cresc.

seek Thee my Life, I tar - - ry, with
Be - hold Me, thy Life, Behold Me!
cresc.
lamp e - ver burn-ing.
f
d
mp
O
mp
I show thee My face,
p

show me Thy face,
O show me Thy face,
cresc.
I show thee My face,
My
cresc.
f
mp
e
cresc.
Thy mer-cy and grace, Come, Je - su,
Come,
f
mf
mer-cy and grace, My mer - cy and grace,
Be - hold Me,
e
cresc.
p
f
Je - su,
Come, Je - - - su!
cresc.
f
Be - hold Me,
Be-hold Me, I am thy Sal-va-tion!
p

poco cresc.
mp
I
p
f
mp
O show me Thy face, O
show thee My face, I show thee My face,
f

mp
show me Thy face, Thy mercy and grace, Come,
cresc.
My mer-cy and grace, My mer - cy and grace,
cresc.
g
cresc.
Je-su, Come, Je-su, Come,
mf
cresc.
Be - hold Me, Be - hold Me,
g
mp
Je - - su! I
f
Behold Me, I am thy Sal-va-tion!
mf

h
seek Thee, my Life,
I
mf
Be - - hold Me, thy Life,
h
p
seek Thee, my Life,
mf
I seek Thee, my
Be - hold Me, thy Life,
Be - hold Me,
i
Life, my Life!
mp
I tar - - ry, I
thy Life,
thy Life,
Behold Me, thy
i

poco cresc.
tar - - ry, I tar - - - - -
poco cresc.
Life, Be - hold Me, Be - hold Me,
poco cresc.
k
poco dim.
- - - - - - - - - ry, with
poco dim.
Be - hold Me, thy Life, Be - hold Me, thy
k
mf
poco dim.
poco cresc.
f
lamp e - ver burn - ing, with lamp e - ver burn-ing, I
f
Life, Be - hold Me, thy Life,
poco cresc.

1

seek Thee, My Life! I tar - - ry, with

Be-hold Me, thy Life, Be-hold Me!

1

lamp e - ver burn-ing.

mf

p

poco cresc.

mf

poco dim.

CHORALE. Verse II.
Vl. & Viola.
♩=80. f
p
f
tr
A
TENOR. (Tutti.)
f
Zi - on hears her watch-men's voi - - ces, Their

B
gladd'ning cry her soul re-joi - - - ces
C
The sha - dows of her night de - part.
f
p
f
tr
tr
tr
tr

D

In His might her Lord ap-pear-eth,

E

His word of grace and truth she hear-eth,

F

The day-star ri-seth in her heart.

G
O
H
come, in splen - dour bright,
Lord Je - su,
I
Light of Light!
Ho - si - an - - -
- na!
tr
p
mf
p
cresc.

K
We fol - low Thee,
Thy joy to see,
L
Where e - ver - last - ing bliss shall be.
f
mf
tr
cresc.

RECITATIVE.

* Bar 8. Possibly G natural.

AIR. (DUET.)
Ob.
SOPRANO.
My Friend is mine!
BASS.
And
Our love no pow'r shall sun - - der.
I am thine! Our love no pow'r shall sun - der, nought sun - der.

SOPRANO.
mf
n
My Friend is mine! Our
BASS.
mf
And I am thine! Our
p
n
love no pow'r shall sun - - der, my Friend is mine,
love no pow'r shall sun-der, nought sun-der, and
piano sempre
o
my Friend is mine, my Friend is mine,
I am thine, and I am thine, and I am
o

p
our love no pow'r shall sun - der, my Friend is
thine, our love no pow'r shall sun - der, and
p
mine, our love no pow'r shall sun - der, my Friend is
I am thine, and I am thine, and
mine, our love no pow'r shall sun - der, our love no
I am thine, and I am thine, our love

cresc.
pow'r shall sun - - - - der, our love no
cresc.
no pow'r shall sun - - der, our love
cresc.
q
mf
pow'r shall sun - - - der, my Friend is mine,
tr
mf
no pow'r shall sun - - der, and I am
q
p
cresc.
our love no pow'r shall sun - der.
tr
cresc.
tr
thine, our love no pow'r shall sun - - der.
f

SOPRANO.
mp
Thou lead - est me, Thou lead - est me, by
BASS.
mp
Thus lead I thee, thus lead I
p
heav'n - ly streams to wan - - der, Thou
thee by heav'n - - ly streams to wan - - - -

lead - est — me, Thou lead - est — me by
- - der, — thus lead — I — thee, thus lead — I —
heav'n - ly — streams — to wan - - - -
thee by heav'n-ly streams — to
- - - - der, — Thou lead - est me,
wan - - der, thus lead I thee by
S
S

cresc.
by heav'nly streams to wan -
cresc.
heav'n-ly streams to wan -
cresc.
f
- der, there joy in its ful-ness, there
f
- der, there joy in its ful-ness, there
mf
mf
t
rap-ture shall be, there joy in its ful-ness,
mf
rap-ture shall be,
there
t

Da Capo dal Segno al 𝄐

CHORALE. Verse III.
SOPRANO.
Glo-ry now to Thee be giv - - en, On earth as in the high-est hea - - ven. With lute and harp in sweetest tone.
All of pearl each dazz-ling por - - tal, Where we shall join the song im - mor - - tal, Of Saints and An-gels round Thy throne.
ALTO.
Glo-ry now to Thee be giv - - en, On earth as in the high-est hea - - ven. With lute and harp in sweetest tone.
All of pearl each dazz-ling por - - tal, Where we shall join the song im - mor - - tal, Of Saints and An-gels round Thy throne.
TENOR.
Glo-ry now to Thee be giv - - en, On earth as in the high-est hea - - ven. With lute and harp in sweetest tone.
All of pearl each dazz-ling por - - tal, Where we shall join the song im - mor - - tal, Of Saints and An-gels round Thy throne.
BASS.
Glo - - ry now to Thee be giv - - en, On earth as in the high-est hea - - ven. With lute and harp in sweetest tone.
All of pearl each dazz-ling por - - tal, Where we shall join the song im - mor - - tal, Of Saints and An-gels round Thy throne.

Printed and bound in Great Britain by
Caligraving Limited Thetford Norfolk